WHAT AM I?

VERY FIRST RIDDLES

by Stephanie Calmenson

Illustrated by Karen Gundersheimer

VIKING

To Jane Feder

S. C.

*To Jay and Rubens
with love*

K.G.

VIKING

Published by the Penguin Group
27 Wrights Lane, London W8 5TZ, England
Viking Penguin Inc., 40 West 23rd Street, New York, New York 10010, USA
Penguin Books Australia Ltd, Ringwood, Victoria, Australia
Penguin Books Canada Ltd, 2801 John Street, Markham, Ontario, Canada L3R 1B4
Penguin Books (NZ) Ltd, 182–190 Wairau Road, Auckland 10, New Zealand

Penguin Books Ltd, Registered Offices: Harmondsworth, Middlesex, England

First published in the USA by Harper & Row 1989
First published in Great Britain by Viking 1990
1 3 5 7 9 10 8 6 4 2

Text copyright © Stephanie Calmenson, 1989
Illustrations copyright © Karen Gundersheimer, 1989

Printed in Hong Kong by Imago

A CIP catalogue record for this book is available from the British Library

ISBN 0–670–83335–3

Tick, tick, tick
Is the sound I make,
Or ring, ring, ring
To help you wake.

What am I?

A clock.

To guess what I am
Is easy as can be.
Your sock goes on your foot
And your foot goes into me.

What am I?

A shoe.

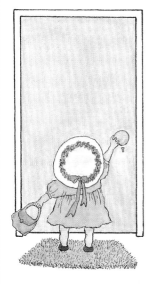

Though we jingle and jangle,

That's not what we're for.

You need one of us

To unlock your door.

What are we?

Keys.

I ring until you pick me up.

You hold me to your ear.

Then someone who is far away

Seems to be right here.

What am I?

A telephone.

I hang from a bar,
Or sometimes a tree.
Ask a friend for a push
When you ride on me.

What am I?

A swing.

You'll find us on your birthday cake,
Each one of us aglow.
Close your eyes and make a wish,
Then take a breath and blow!

What are we?

Candles.

We're pretty to look at
And nice to smell.
If you have a garden,
You know us well.

What are we?

Flowers.

I have three wheels
And a horn to blow.
Just pedal, pedal,
Then off we go.

What am I?

A tricycle.

When rain comes falling
Down from the sky,
Open me up
If you want to stay dry.

What am I?

An umbrella.

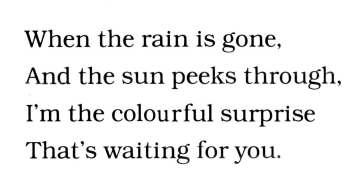

When the rain is gone,
And the sun peeks through,
I'm the colourful surprise
That's waiting for you.

What am I?

A rainbow.

Dip the wand
And gently blow.
Off we sail,
Then POP! we go.

What are we?

Bubbles.

I have string and a tail,
And I'm made to fly.
On a breezy day,
See me up in the sky.

What am I?

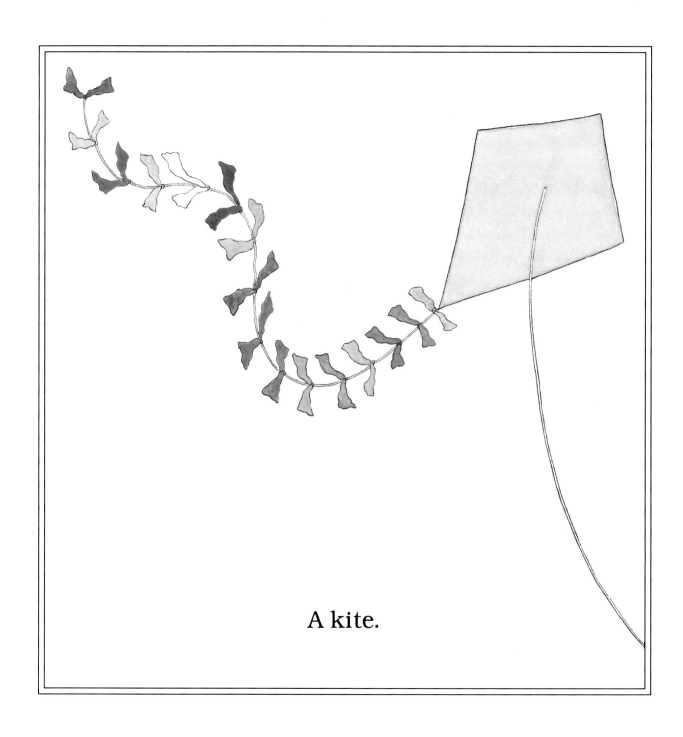

A kite.

I'm sweet and cold,

So take a lick.

But watch me melt

If you're not quick!

What am I?

Ice cream.

Listen to me! Listen to me!
Clickety-clack!
Watch for me! Watch for me!
Coming down the track.

What am I?

A train.

You're almost at the end of me.

Just one more page to go.

I hope you'll share me with a friend.

What am I? Do you know?

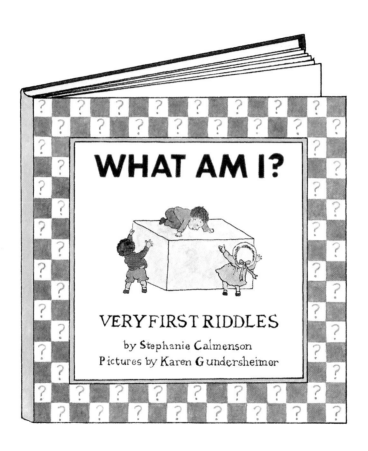

A book.